God is Kind

God is Kind

A children's book produced by
The Bible Tells Me So Press

Copyright © 2019
The Bible Tells Me So Corporation

All rights reserved. No part of this book, neither text nor illustrations, may be reproduced without permission in writing by the publisher.

PUBLISHED BY
THE BIBLE TELLS ME SO CORPORATION
WWW.THEBIBLETELLSMESO.COM

First Printing July, 2019

for all that He's made.

and animals shade.

and brings up the sun

He gives flowers to bees

and honey to bears,

He cares when you smile

God's big and He's strong,

Yes, you're...

on His mind.

For Jehovah is good;
His lovingkindness is forever...

Psalm 100:5a

For more
books, videos, songs, and crafts,
visit us online at
TheBibleTellsMeSo.com

Standing on the Bible and growing!